CHARTING
A COURSE

ACQUISITION STRATEGIES
IN THE GREEN INDUSTRY

RON EDMONDS
The Principium Group

ISBN: 1479311677
ISBN-13: 978-1479311675

DEDICATION

This book is dedicated to Pouncer who has taught me it is OK to love a dog again, even if she is named after a cat.

Also by Ron Edmonds

Green Exit – Exit Planning for Lawn and Landscape Business Owners

How to Sell Your Green Business – A Guide for Green Industry Business Owner

CONTENTS

ACKNOWLEDGMENTS

I truly appreciate the influence and encouragement I have received to continue writing on subjects related to the green industry by clients, fellow consultants and others within the green industry.

My friend Jeffrey Scott of The Leader's Edge Peer Group inspired me to have the owner of the fictional company featured in this narrative participate in a peer group. I have been very impressed by the power of peer group participation in driving business performance and accountability.

I am once again eternally grateful for the support and encouragement of my partner, editor and proofreader, Kathryn Edmonds. Her efforts have greatly improved the final product

FOREWORD

This book is intended as an introduction to thinking about acquisitions for lawn and landscape business owners and others in the green industry.

We began a project about a year ago to prepare a guidebook for green industry acquisitions. That book will be entitled *Green Acquisitions – A Growth Strategy for Lawn and Landscape Business Owners.* It is expected to be published in 2013.

This book, *Charting a Course –Acquisition Strategies in the Green Industry,* includes excerpts from *Green Acquisitions* and is intended to be a simple introduction to the growth strategies that can be impacted by business acquisitions.

We hope that *Charting a Course* will whet your appetite for more and that you will want a copy of *Green Acquisitions* when it is published. *Green Acquisitions* will cover much more ground, including the steps in executing an acquisition growth strategy.

We believe that we are in one of those unique times that the opportunities to accelerate growth with strategic acquisitions is particularly strong. There is a greater than typical supply of business owners who are willing to consider selling or merging their businesses as well as progressive business owners interested in considering acquisitions. In the words of a friend of mine, "These are the times in which great companies are built."

1

INTRODUCTION

Few business issues are as controversial as the role of business acquisitions in facilitating and stimulating business growth.

There is a natural preference for so-called organic growth, growth that comes from the existing business without the benefit of acquisitions. In fact, organic growth is highly desirable, if it can be achieved at reasonable cost and within a reasonable timeframe. This is not always the case. Although it may seem somewhat counter-intuitive, sometimes acquisitions can be a more cost-effective and less risky strategy for generating business growth than relying on organic growth.

That does not mean that growing by acquisitions is an easy process. It is not. Widely-reported statistics suggest that many acquisitions fail to deliver the expected value to the acquiring business. In fact, some studies indicate that acquisitions can destroy value instead of building it.

However, there is definitely a role in many businesses for acquisitions in accelerating growth, reaching critical mass, achieving market leadership and breaking through barriers to growth that arise at various points in a business's life cycle.

This book tells the story of a mythical landscape services company, The Vivant Landscape Team, owned by a mythical owner, Philo Sanders, with a mythical management team.

While Vivant has been incredibly successful in its first 10 years of operations, its owner believes that growth will be much more difficult in the future. Philo is a forward-thinking leader in the green industry, who has been thinking about ways to stimulate growth. One of the things he has done is to discuss the situation with the members of his peer group, a group of mostly like-minded green industry business owners in noncompetitive markets who meet regularly to learn from each other and hold each other accountable.

In this story, Philo takes the idea of acquisitions to Vivant's management team. The team brings a variety of perspectives to the possibility of an acquisition. Each member of the Vivant management team makes his or her pitch for the kind of acquisition he or she believes will be most beneficial for The Vivant Landscape Team.

Using input from the management team, professional advisors and members of the peer group, Philo and his CFO develop a checklist for the preliminary evaluation of acquisition opportunities. We hope you will find their checklist helpful in your business.

We also include an in-depth discussion of growth strategies for the green industry and how acquisitions can play a significant role in many situations.

2

INTRODUCING VIVANT
LANDSCAPE

Philo was excited about the day ahead. Vivant Landscape had never really had a strategic planning meeting before. As he pulled his truck into the parking lot of the country club where he'd reserved a room for the day, he could not help reflecting on how he and Vivant Landscape had gotten this far.

Philo Sanders founded Vivant Landscape just over ten years ago. He had worked for a major landscape services company in the Mid-Atlantic for about five years after graduating from Mississippi State where he had completed a degree in landscape architecture. He had received a scholarship to play football at Mississippi State and had gone there to be a running back for the Bulldogs. He played a lot his sophomore through senior years. He had chosen Mississippi State because it was his best shot to get some playing time in the powerhouse Southeastern Conference.

His family and his high school coach had thought the NFL might be in his future, but he had had lots of doubts. He had not wanted to be one of those guys whose life was built around sports and then didn't know what to do if he weren't quite good enough to make it in the pros, or a relatively minor injury cut short an otherwise promising career.

When he arrived in Starkville, he didn't know what he wanted to major in, but he knew that whatever it was, he would take it very seriously. He discovered that MSU had a well-known landscape architecture program. After further investigation, he settled on the landscape contracting and management program for his college major. His college football coaches were extremely discouraging to him about his choice of a major. They reminded him of the time commitment he had made to the football program. They thought the landscape program would be too challenging to manage. In fact, no one on the athletic staff at MSU could even remember a varsity football player who had completed the major - ever. The academic success of their scholarship players was an important goal of the coaches, and the last thing they wanted was for a promising athlete to choose a major he was unlikely to succeed in. If they had known just a little bit more about Philo, they would have known that trying to discourage him by suggesting he probably wouldn't be successful in the landscape program only motivated him more.

To be honest, the director of the landscape program wasn't too thrilled about a football player either. He thought the student-player might expect a lot of breaks and that the department might even be under pressure from the coaches to let the player slide a little. He and the faculty were very proud of the reputation they had built for producing highly skilled, motivated graduates. He didn't want to do anything that might lessen that reputation or let his department be placed in a compromising position.

But when the director met Philo, he knew that he would be a serious student. Philo knew something about the landscape management business, having spent two summers working for a contractor back home.

By the time his senior year came around, everyone in the landscape program took him seriously. Any idea he might be drafted by the NFL had been forgotten, but he was a top student in landscape management. He had successfully juggled the obligations of a Division 1-A football player with the requirements of one of the most challenging majors on campus. He was heavily recruited. He had been sponsored to attend the Professional Landscape Network's Student Career Days at Kansas State University where he had the opportunity to meet recruiters from numerous landscape services companies. He had been offered the chance to attend Planet's Green Industry Conference, but that was out of the question since it was in the middle of football season.

After interviews with several companies, he settled on a large regional company which had a branch not far from his hometown. Once again, his drive and ambition served him well, and he was soon one of the youngest, if not the youngest, branch manager in the company. There was definitely a solid career path for him there, but the entrepreneur spirit had been planted in him long ago, and he knew he would soon be ready to start his own business.

He had carefully saved money, including all of the bonuses he had received. With his nest egg and some additional funding from his family, he launched his own company. He named it Vivant Landscape Team. He liked the sound of "vivant." To him it was the perfect name for a landscape company since it means "living" in French. In a sense, "team" reflected his sports background, but he really used it because he knew it would take the right team to make his business successful. He did not have that team in place yet, but seeing the name would always remind him of the importance of developing the right one.

The first couple of years were pretty tough, requiring him to work nearly every day during the season and wear many different hats, but soon the business took off. By the end of five years in business, Vivant's annual revenues had grown to about $3 million with 40 employees. Five years later, he had hit another milestone, $10 million in revenue and 135 employees. He could hardly believe it. He was 37 years old, and he had cracked the bottom of those Top 100 and Top 150 lists.

He had a terrific team in place. Robert Colbert was vice president of maintenance operations. Richard Cartman was vice president of design-build operations. Ben Waxman was vice president of sales. The newest member of the team was Stephen Peebles, his CFO. He was amazed that he owned a company that needed a chief financial officer. His other key employee was Rachel Speer. Rachel had been his first administrative employee and had been with him for ten years now. She was in every sense his assistant, but she also handled human resources for the company, a pretty big challenge for a company with 135 employees.

Philo considered his participation in professional organizations, including the state landscaping association and The Professional Landcare Network (Planet) to be one of the keys to his success. Even more important was his participation in a peer group. He was a member of a group of five owners of similar businesses in different markets who met three times a year to exchange information about their businesses, including their successes and their challenges. The peer group could be pretty tough. There was a sense of accountability there that was difficult to maintain as the sole owner of a business. He got some great ideas there, too. For example, it was his peer group colleagues that convinced him it was time to have his own CFO. Boy, were they right! That one decision seemed like it had made all the difference in the world. With better data in hand and his own, in-house advisor, he was making much better decisions about all facets of the business, including what kind of new business to take on and how much to spend on new equipment. Most importantly, he had brought professionalism to managing cash flow, always one of Philo's greatest challenges. Philo no longer lost sleep worrying about making payroll even though his business was growing rapidly.

Having built a strong business and a strong team, Philo was ready to begin planning for the future.

Introducing Vivant Landscape

3

THE TEAM

Philo was very proud of the management team he had developed for Vivant Landscape. They came from a variety of backgrounds and had a variety of skills. They complemented each other in a way that made the company much stronger than the sum of its parts.

Robert Colbert was vice president of maintenance operations. Robert was the "old man" of the bunch. He had been in the landscape industry for over 30 years. The last six of those years he had spent with Philo at Vivant. Vivant was the third landscape company he had worked for. He had previously worked for a large regional company and then a much smaller local landscape company. Philo had met him once at a landscape association event. Robert had been very unhappy with his former position. He felt like his employer was not interested in growing. The business had stayed the same size, maybe dropping a little over a three-year period when many other similar companies were growing. Robert had signed with the small company in the hopes it would grow much larger and create a bigger opportunity for him. He felt he was doing his part but that the owner was not really interested in seriously growing his business. The chemistry with Philo was good from the moment they met. When Philo asked if he would be interested in joining Vivant in a management position, Robert jumped at the chance. During the six years he had been with Vivant, Vivant had tripled in size. Philo gave much of the credit for growth to Robert. Robert had a reputation for outstanding service to the company's customers and being a good leader for the company's field employees. He was demanding, but he backed it up by treating his employees very well.

Richard Cartman served as vice president of design-build operations. He had a degree in landscape architecture from The Ohio State University. He was active in designing projects, but much of that work was now performed by the other three landscape designers on his staff. Richard was a true artist and had a great reputation in the community. His team designed both high-end residential projects and commercial ones. The three construction crews also reported to Richard.

Ben Waxman was vice president of sales. His team of three sales people was responsible for sales of both maintenance and design-build operations. Vivant's growth had really begun in earnest after Ben joined the team four and a half years earlier. What was really unique about Ben and his background was that Ben had no experience at all in the landscape business before joining Vivant. When Philo had been looking for a sales manager, he networked around town, and a friend of his from the Kiwanis Club had suggested that he connect with Ben, who had a strong background in business-to-business sales and was looking for a new opportunity. Though Philo was cautious about the idea, when he met Ben, the chemistry was strong, and he never regretted the decision.

Although he was still a young man under thirty, Stephen Peebles had already made his mark on the company as chief financial officer. He was a certified public accountant and worked for a small local CPA firm prior to joining Vivant. Philo's peer group had been insistent that Vivant would really benefit from a strong financial leader. Philo had looked hard, seeking the kind of accountant who would fit into his organization, be respected and bring the talent and drive which would help take Vivant to the next level.

He found that combination in Stephen, and it didn't take long for him to make a real difference. Stephen had been with Vivant for a year and a half now. Philo had been used to seeing financial statements about a month after the end of the month, occasionally longer. He now had them by the tenth of the month, every month. He received some financial information every week, and still other data, like cash flow information, he received every day. Philo now felt like he could make important decisions based on information and facts, instead of just gut instinct. He also had an in-house business advisor on important issues where formerly he would have had to consult with his outside CPA. Now he could just step across the hall – or shout if he felt like it. The changes Stephen had recommended had already improved cash flow significantly. Although many of those changes were pretty simple, like billing at the beginning of the month or requiring deposits, they were actually being enforced, and the results were impressive.

The last member of the management team was Rachel Speer. Rachel had been with Vivant almost since day one. Originally, she was a part time administrative employee while she was in college studying psychology. Actually, she was originally the only administrative employee and the fourth person Philo hired for Vivant. She was a quick study and had a very strong knowledge of all aspects of the business. She remained with Vivant after graduation and still provided administrative support for Philo. She understood him and the business and had his full confidence. Five years earlier, as the business had begun to grow, Philo had asked her to take on human resources functions for the company, a perfect match for her degree studies. She had attended many training programs offered through Planet and other organizations and always tried to stay current on the most recent developments. With 150 employees, even with a high quality and stable workforce, keeping every position filled was still a challenge. Of course, there was also the issue of compliance with all the relevant federal, state and local regulations. It was a big job, and Rachel did it well.

So those were the members of the management committee, five managers plus Philo for a total of six. They held a weekly meeting every Monday morning as soon as crews were dispatched. They were a tight-knit group, and usually everyone on the management team knew what was going on in the company without having to wait for a Monday morning meeting. But Philo was convinced that weekly meetings were the best idea to ensure that everyone communicated and the team was working together. He also asked each of his managers to have a meeting with his or her own teams sometime during the week.

THE TEAM

4

THE MEETING

Philo walked into the country club and found the room he had reserved. The team had already gathered. Stephen, Richard, Ben, Robert and Rachel had gathered around the coffee pot. They greeted Philo when he entered the room and then took seats around the table.

Philo thanked them all for joining him. He proceeded to describe the purpose of the meeting and became a bit philosophical as he reflected on how far Vivant Landscape had come in its short ten years of existence. They had posted a record $10 million in revenues in the last year, despite pretty challenging economic times. Just yesterday, he had received a call from the editor of *Landscape Management* magazine, who had informed him that Vivant would rank number 99 on its annual ranking of the top landscape contractors in the United States. The list would be published in the next month's issue. She interviewed him for an article on newcomers to the list which would appear in the same issue.

Just two weeks ago, Philo had handed out bonuses to his management team, reflecting their role in achieving the growth in the business. Most of the team members had been a little startled – and pleased – about how rewarding their careers at Vivant had become.

Philo said that he had been giving a great deal of thought to how well the company had performed over the past few years and the progress they had made. He said their growth had been very good and that it was growth that had made Vivant such a good place to work. And not just for the management team: The profitable growth they had experienced had created opportunities for just about everyone in the company who had been seeking career advancement.

What was troubling him was that he believed that the level of growth they had achieved so far would be very hard to sustain in the coming years. While they had a great reputation, the marketplace had become extremely competitive, and the economy had continued to be very choppy. They would have to be innovative and aggressive to continue to grow at anything like the pace they had seen the last five years.

One strategy he had been thinking about was acquisitions. One of the members of his peer group had made several successful acquisitions that had enabled his company to sustain its momentum in its marketplace, and that was an idea that Philo was interested in at least considering.

He had brought the group together to consider the possibilities.

Stephen asked Philo exactly what kind of acquisitions he was thinking about. With his accountant's mind, the questions flowed:

What kind of acquisition did he have in mind?

What synergies was he expecting?

How big an acquisition did Philo think they could pull off?

How would it be financed?

Philo looked at the group and the confusion in their faces. Reflecting a bit, he said, "At this point, let's think about the possibilities, not the details of how big or how it might be financed. If those kinds of issues don't matter, what kind of acquisitions should we consider as we plan what Vivant Landscape might look like in the future?"

He asked each one of his management team members what kind of acquisitions he or she might consider if the decision were up to them.

After he let them all think for a few minutes, he went around the room and asked for their initial thoughts.

Richard Cartman, the vice president of design-build services, spoke up first. He said he would like to see

Vivant acquire a similar company in a nearby city to expand the universe of potential customers.

Ben Waxman, the vice president of sales, said he would like to see Vivant acquire a company that added to the product and service lines provided by Vivant. He suggested an irrigation company or perhaps a swimming pool company. That way, Vivant could sell more to existing customers.

Stephen said he would like to acquire a company that could quickly be integrated into Vivant to cut costs.

Robert Colbert, the vice president of maintenance operations, said he would like to see Vivant acquire a local company to expand the customer base and allow the maintenance crews to become more efficient and cut costs. Hopefully, it would allow for tighter routes and less drive time, thereby improving labor efficiency and reducing fuel costs.

Rachel spoke up with a different idea. She thought Vivant should buy a garden center and use it as a location to sell landscape design/build services from. Vivant could have hardscape displays and that kind of thing.

Philo was absolutely amazed at what he heard. No two members of his management team came up with the same kind of acquisition they should pursue, but they agreed that an acquisition might be a very good idea.

The range of ideas that had been thrown out absolutely intrigued him. After thinking about the responses he had received, he concluded that all of them made at least some sense. He decided that he would adjourn their meeting for one week with an assignment for each member of the management team. Each one was asked to come to next week's meeting prepared to defend why his or her recommendation of an acquisition target was appropriate and to identify at least two businesses in the category that they recommended to pursue.

With the assignments announced, Philo called for a waiter, and they ordered lunch.

5

ONE WEEK LATER

When Philo pulled up to the country club the next week, he was excited to find out what the team had come up with. While they all had been pretty tight-lipped about their ideas during the past week, it was obvious they were taking on the assignment with enthusiasm. He knew from experience that when this team took on something with enthusiasm and the passion they all shared, anything was possible.

The meeting would be in the same room this week. The team was already there, with each one looking back over their notes in anticipation of their presentations. After Philo greeted them all and took his own seat, he reminded them of the ground rules. They were all here to consider the possibilities. He had not ruled out any of their ideas. There was a lot to learn and consider about each idea, and today was another step in the process. He asked them all to allow each team member to make his or her presentation without interrupting with questions. Those should be saved for the end. With that, he called on Robert Colbert to make the first presentation.

Robert Colbert proposed that the most logical acquisition for them to make was another local landscape maintenance company. His basic theory was that adding a maintenance company that operated in the same area would significantly strengthen Vivant in some key ways. It would add to the recurring revenue component of the business that added value, strength and stability to the company. If the acquisition were primarily commercial maintenance, it would also support their key thrusts in growing the commercial business.

Robert passed around an analysis he'd prepared of the impact of both drive-time and fuel costs on Vivant's profitability. The report indicated that if they could acquire a maintenance company with approximately the same geographic footprint that added perhaps 30% to the maintenance division's business, he could grow profits by nearly 50% by improving route efficiency. That was a percentage that everyone took note of. One other thing Robert mentioned was that he hoped an acquisition could bring in some pretty good people. They all knew what a challenge it was to identify, recruit and retain good people in the business these days.

As Robert wrapped up his well thought out presentation, Philo asked if he had any suggestions of companies they might consider as acquisition targets. Robert had three in mind. He believed each had about $1 million in maintenance revenues. Philo and a couple of the others flinched a little when Robert mentioned the names of his proposed acquisition targets, not so much because they had anything negative to say about them, but because they had competed so vigorously against them. Much discussion among the team followed as they considered different aspects of pursuing an acquisition of one of these competitors. Robert was prepared for everything they asked.

After thanking Robert for his presentation, Philo called on Richard Cartman, the vice president of design-build operations, to make the next presentation.

Richard had a little different perspective. He had proposed that they consider acquiring a similar company to their own in a nearby town. His theory was that an acquisition of this type would expand the universe of customers for them to sell design-build services to. They could also grow the whole company. Unlike the company's recurring maintenance business, much of the design-build sales were to new customers, and each project had to be sold individually, whether or not if it were to an existing Vivant customer. Even with selling costs for each project, design-build could be a highly profitable business segment

Richard, too, had prepared an analysis. His analysis suggested that if they could acquire a company perhaps one-third to one-half their size in a nearby community within a 30-mile radius, they would have a new beachhead and would still be able to eliminate many duplicated overhead costs. Customer retention should be better, too, since they could probably cast the transaction as a merger instead of a sale of the business. It was also possible that they could find an acquisition target that might have strengths that would improve Vivant's existing operations. On the other hand, there would likely be areas of the target's business that Vivant could improve after the acquisition, increasing the acquisition's contribution to the combined companies' sales and profits.

After Richard was through, Philo asked him for any potential targets he had identified. He had three as well, but oddly, none of the other management team members recognized any of them.

After additional discussion and a coffee break, Philo called on Ben Waxman for his thoughts. Ben, the sales vice president, had recommended considering acquiring a complementary business. His theory was simple, but rather persuasive. He was thinking about products and services that their existing customers needed and used, but Vivant did not currently offer. He had come up with three possibilities: irrigation system design, installation and maintenance; swimming pool design, construction and maintenance; and outdoor living furniture and equipment. There was another angle on this option as well: Companies providing any of these services would have many customers who needed the landscape services Vivant already provided. The opportunities for cross-selling might be enormous. Ben actually had some real data to work with, too. Of their high-end residential maintenance customers, twelve had installed swimming pools in the last year. That was nearly $1 million in revenue going to somebody else. Half of those customers had actually sought out Vivant's recommendation of a swimming pool contractor. Eighty percent of their maintenance customers had irrigation systems. Much of that business came through Vivant, but they subcontracted it out to one of three irrigation contractors they worked with. He estimated their customers spent at least $500,000 on irrigation maintenance and service annually and as much as $1 million on irrigation system installations. Outdoor furniture was another area that seemed promising because they were installing many outdoor living rooms and kitchens for their upscale residential clients. Anyone who spent a substantial amount on one of these projects must be spending a great deal on outdoor furniture as well. The company's designers often made specific furniture recommendations and included them in their drawings, but Vivant wasn't harvesting any of the revenues.

Everyone found Ben's presentation extremely interesting. When Philo asked him for potential targets, the list was a little different: Everyone knew the names and knew them well. They weren't competitors or in an unfamiliar city; they did business together regularly.

Philo called on Rachel next for her presentation on the possibility of acquiring a garden center. This idea was different as well. No one had really thought about this possibility or what it might involve or lead to. Rachel pointed out that many successful landscaping companies in other cities had design centers that customers could come to. The purpose of a design center was two-fold. First, it was a place where a design-build customer or potential customer could come and meet with a designer. Customers would have on-site access to the designer's computer-based drafting tools to see what a project might look like. They also had a variety of actual landscape installations on the premises of the design center to show what a project might actually look like after it was completed. It didn't eliminate the need to visit the homeowner's residence to complete the drawings and the plans, but it really produced a compelling sales system. While no one in their town was using the design center concept, she had met several contractors at trade shows who used the concept successfully and were enthusiastic advocates. Acquiring a garden center could allow them to establish a design center in an existing business that had its own revenues and profits. She said there would be a real opportunity for cross-selling, too. The garden center's existing customers would be potential customers for design-build and maintenance. Their existing customers might also become garden center customers.

Philo asked her if she had identified any garden centers that would be potential targets; she said that she had. Many of the garden centers in town were seasonal businesses that disappeared over the winter months. She did not think those would be good targets for acquisition. There were three, however, that she thought might be worth pursuing. All three had been around for years, and they all knew them. One in particular they knew well because its owners frequently referred their customers seeking a landscaper to Vivant.

Now it was Stephen's turn. Philo and Stephen had spoken shortly after last week's meeting. Stephen did not have a particular kind of acquisition he was recommending, but he did have some thoughts to share with the group about factors they should consider in identifying potential targets, and Philo had asked Stephen to share his thoughts with the rest of the team.

In Stephen's mind, a good acquisition for Vivant was one that could be had at a reasonable valuation, could be integrated fairly quickly and had the opportunity to reduce the costs of the combined company, making them more efficient and competitive in the marketplace.

Stephen then led a discussion on what he meant by integration. He listed off many of the items that would have to be addressed in any integration plan. Among the issues he included were:

- Branding and identity
- Facilities integration
- Management structure and employee team integration
- Human resource issues
- Sales process and pricing strategies
- Accounting systems
- Credit policies

That list was just a start. The final list would in all likelihood be very long and detailed. This discussion raised a question in everyone's mind whether there was any kind of acquisition that could be "integrated fairly quickly."

Philo thanked Stephen for his contribution and opened the floor for discussion. Everyone had questions for each other, and the discussion was lively. After about 30 minutes, Philo announced that the discussion would continue in the room next door over drinks and snacks. It was two hours before everyone headed home thinking about next steps in studying acquisitions for Vivant.

6

NEXT STEPS

Philo had given a great deal of thought to the proposals from each member of his management team. He was glad that he had a peer group meeting coming up and planned to ask for feedback from other members of his peer group, some of whom had completed acquisitions of their own.

At the peer group meeting, Philo asked for a few minutes to discuss acquisitions and get feedback from the group. While one member of the group couldn't understand why anyone would consider an acquisition, most of the others were more enthusiastic. Several had completed acquisitions, and several others either had considered them in the past or were actively considering them now.

Some of the common themes included in their comments were as follows:

- Be realistic in your expectations.
- Build your acquisition assumptions based on the possibility of things not going perfectly.
- Don't bite off more than your team can handle.

- Consider the risks you are taking on.
- Be sure to plan your integration strategy before you complete the acquisition.

One of the most important things he took away from that meeting was the need to assemble a team of people inside the company along with outside advisors who would be responsible for making up the acquisition team.

When he returned home, he began the process of talking with his key advisors. He visited with his outside accountant and his attorney. His accountant asked him to keep him in the loop on discussions as they developed to make sure tax consequences were appropriately addressed. His attorney, who had been with him nearly since he started Vivant, told him that he had handled very few business acquisition transactions, and it might be a good idea to bring in another attorney for that purpose. He promised to make some inquiries and introductions. At his peer group meeting, Philo had also gotten the names of a couple of merger & acquisition advisors who specialized in the landscape industry that other members of the peer group used. He called them to discuss their services and what he had in mind.

His next stop was his banker whom he knew very well. He told him he did not have a deal on the table right now, but wanted to talk about how a transaction might be financed, including what might be possible, what the underwriting process entailed and how long it might take.

Philo wasn't really in a hurry to pursue a deal right now, but when an opportunity came his way, he wanted to be ready. He was covering his bases.

Back at the office, he sat down with Stephen, his CFO, and together they came up with a list of questions they would ask in evaluating any potential acquisition before beginning the due diligence process in earnest.

Here is the list they came up with:

PRELIMINARY ACQUISITION EVALUATION CHECKLIST

1. How does the proposed acquisition address the company's strategic objectives?

2. Is the acquisition big enough to justify the financial and managerial resources required to negotiate and close a transaction and develop and implement an effective transition plan?

3. Does there appear to be a cultural fit between the company and the prospective target?

4. Is there a high probability that the target company's key employees can be retained after the acquisition?

5. Is there a high probability that the target company's customers can be retained after the acquisition?

6. What impact will the proposed acquisition have on the company's existing employees?

7. What impact will the proposed acquisition have on the company's existing customer base?

8. Is it likely that the target company can be acquired at a valuation that is reasonable and is likely to produce a solid return on investment for the company?

9. Are there any positive or negative trends in the potential target's business or industry sector that should affect the company's evaluation or level of interest in the acquisition?

10. Are there obvious tax issues that should affect the company's evaluation or level of interest in the acquisition?

11. Does the company have the financial resources and strength to complete the proposed acquisition without compromising other operations and plans?

12. Does the company have the human resources available to go through the due

diligence, acquisition and integration processes?

13. How does the proposed acquisition compare to other possible acquisitions or other investment opportunities in terms of anticipated return on investment and fit with the company's strategic objectives?

14. What new risks would the proposed acquisition expose the company to?

15. What new risks would the proposed acquisition expose the acquired company to?

Next Steps

7

AFTERWORD

Our goal in this book has been to put the subject of acquisitions for green industry companies in some perspective. We chose to tell a story, the story of The Vivant Landscape Team, its owner, Philo Sanders, and its management team.

While Vivant has not yet decided to make an acquisition, they are thinking about the opportunities that may exist in or near their market to grow their business in one of several ways by making a strategic acquisition. By pooling the thoughts and resources of the management team with those of Philo's peer group members and his professional advisors, Philo has created a structure for making a preliminary evaluation of a potential acquisition target to make a decision as to whether the company may want to pursue the acquisition of a target business. The next steps would involve reaching out to the target, negotiations, due diligence, and if a decision were made to proceed, the development of an integration plan, the drafting of a definitive agreement and actually completing the acquisition and integrating it into their existing operations. Those are topics for another book.

We think the Preliminary Acquisition Evaluation Checklist they came up with is a useful document that green industry business owners may want to use.

The appendix to this book, Acquisition Strategy, includes a discussion of the different approaches to growth strategy: increasing market share, adding new services or products, entering new markets and adding new products or services in new markets. Those strategies are illustrated in the Ansoff Matrix. Any of those strategies might include acquisitions. We hope that reviewing this information will help business owners and managers focus their growth strategy.

Overall, we have attempted to illustrate situations in which strategic acquisitions may represent a logical path to follow when pursuing growth, along with the thought processes that should be involved in making a decision to proceed.

AFTERWORD

APPENDIX:
ACQUISITION STRATEGY

It is a popular belief that all businesses, including small businesses, must grow to thrive. While many of our beliefs about business have been challenged over the past four years, and only a few businesses have been able to sustain growth during the Great Recession, growth is a major objective for many, if not most, businesses.

There are multiple reasons for the "growth imperative," all of which may apply to businesses in the green industry: Growth is often a factor in creating long-term value for the owners of the business; sustained and projected growth is a major factor in creating a sellable business as part of an exit strategy; growth can be necessary to create opportunities for the team and allow the business to recruit and retain top talent; and pursuing a growth strategy encourages innovation and helps keep the business ahead of the evolving competitive landscape.

There are a number of ways to pursue growth. The "growth strategy matrix" which follows is one way to analyze the possibilities for pursuing business growth:

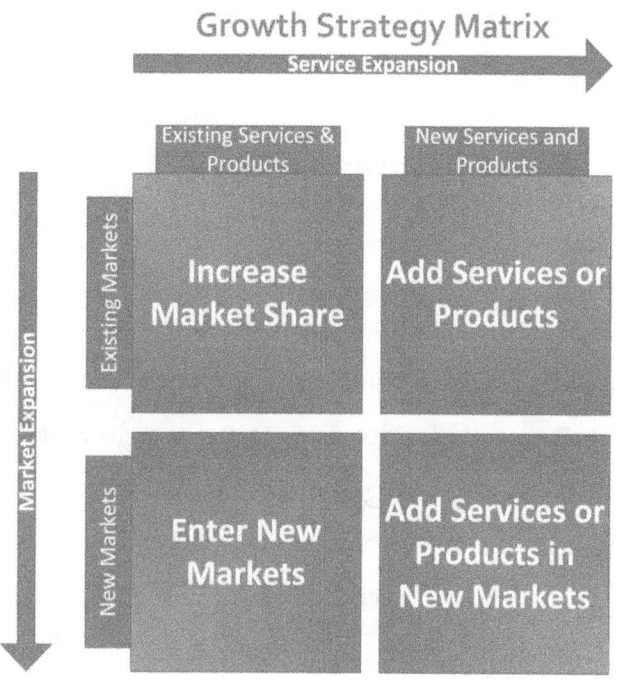

The growth strategy matrix breaks down growth opportunities into two broad categories, market expansion and service (or product) expansion.

Market expansion is further broken down into increasing market share within existing markets and entering new markets. Service expansion can also be further broken down into adding services or products within existing markets and adding services or products in new markets.

Arithmetically, that about does it for strategies to increase revenues.

Each of the four strategies illustrated on the matrix can be attempted either organically or using acquisitions. Organic growth is often considered to be desirable, especially if there is an opportunity to achieve it within the time and resource constraints of the business. Using acquisitions as a tool to achieve growth can also be highly attractive for a number of reasons. A company can often reduce the risk of either market or service expansion by using strategic acquisitions that allow the company to add services or products or new markets without incurring losses during the expansion period.

Some examples of how the four growth strategies can involve acquisitions follow:

Increase Market Share

Acquisitions made for the purpose of increasing market share tend to work best for companies that have a high proportion of recurring revenues, such as lawn care and landscape maintenance businesses. An acquiring company in these cases has a shot at retaining a significant portion of the recurring revenue of the acquired business after the transaction is completed, thereby increasing its market share. It still isn't easy, of course, but there is a definite opportunity.

Companies that do not have a high proportion of recurring revenue are usually not candidates for acquisition if the goal is building market share. This would be the typical situation for a landscape design-build company. In the typical case, once the acquired company's identity is folded into the acquiring company, its position as an alternative provider of the service may be expected to fade away. The acquiring company would likely pick up some new business resulting from the acquisition, but much of it would probably be split among competitors. In a simple case in which there are five competitors in a market and each has a 20% market share, if one competitor buys another one, it might expect their market share to approach 40% (20% for the acquiring company plus 20% from the acquired company). In reality, they might end up with as low as a 25% market share, with the acquired company's new business split roughly evenly among the four remaining competitors.

Enter New Markets

Acquisitions made to enter new markets can make a lot of sense for both recurring revenue and non-recurring revenue businesses. This can be described as selling services to an expanded market, either geographically or defined some other way, such as residential versus commercial.

If a landscape services company acquires a similar business in an adjacent market, there is a greater opportunity to retain customers, since essentially the same business will continue under new ownership. The main difference after the acquisition is likely to be that the combined company may be able to realize some cost synergies as duplicated services are eliminated. The combined company may also be able to bring a stronger service line to the combined business.

Add Services or Products

Adding services or products is often called service expansion. Suppose a landscape services company acquires a complementary business in the same market, perhaps an irrigation company or a fertilization and weed control company. The outlook for customer retention may improve dramatically. In addition, there may be a real opportunity to generate even more revenues through the synergy of the two companies. The acquiring company will have access to the target company's irrigation customers and may attempt to sell other landscape services to them. They can also attempt to sell irrigation services to their existing landscape services customers. This same phenomenon can easily occur if a landscape services company acquires a design-build company or vice versa. There are lots of other possibilities. For example, recently we have seen a number of landscape companies that have an interest in acquiring swimming pool construction or service businesses.

Add Services or Products in New Markets

The strategy of adding services or products in new markets is sometimes called *diversification*. One green industry example of this strategy would be a landscape design-build company acquiring a landscape maintenance company in another market. Diversification strategies have some opportunity for synergies, but in most cases, the synergy opportunities are, at least initially, more limited. Over time, the acquirer could explore cross-selling options, but it would likely take a longer time to execute than in the case of an in-market acquisition.

As we have illustrated in this discussion, there is a role for growth through acquisitions in addition to organic growth. While acquisitions can definitely play a role in reducing the risks associated with a growth strategy, few would argue that planning on growth through acquisitions is not a risky strategy, too. The risk, however, varies a great deal with what the acquiring company is attempting to accomplish and how the acquisition strategy is executed. A plan to grow through acquisitions requires some strategic thinking, but the opportunities are great. Within the landscape industry, there are opportunities for all kinds of businesses to grow through acquisitions. The key is developing a strategy based on an understanding of exactly what you are trying to accomplish and then executing that strategy in a deliberate fashion.

Author's Note: The Growth Strategy Matrix illustrated in this appendix is adapted from the Ansoff Matrix, developed by Igor Ansoff, which first appeared in print in the Harvard Business Review in June 1957.

ACQUISITION STRATEGY

ABOUT THE AUTHOR

Ron Edmonds is president of The Principium Group, Inc. His practice focuses on mergers & acquisitions and related services, including advising clients on matters related to exit strategy planning and  capital formation. He has extensive background in all phases of the merger & acquisition process. In addition to fourteen years in public accounting, he served as chief financial officer for a company executing a consolidation strategy. He has participated as an advisor or intermediary in well over 300 acquisitions during the past ten years.

He is a frequent author and speaker on topics related to green industry mergers and acquisitions. He is the editor of *Green Industry Merger & Acquisition News*, a monthly newsletter tracking the industry, and SellMyGreenBusiness.com, an informational website. He has been a speaker for continuing education programs for over twenty-five years.

Mr. Edmonds' other books include *Green Exit - Exit Planning for Lawn and Landscape Business Owners, How to Sell Your Green Business - A Guide for Green Industry Business Owners* and *A Toolkit for Selling Your Green Business*.

Mr. Edmonds is an adjunct faculty member of the School of Business at Christian Brothers University. He currently teaches MBA-level courses in Entrepreneurship.

He is a certified public accountant (Oklahoma, inactive) and a member of the Association for Corporate Growth, the Association of Professional Mergers & Acquisitions Advisors, the Professional Landcare Network and the International Business Brokers Association. He holds BS and MS degrees in accounting from the Spears School of Business at Oklahoma State University.

To schedule a consultation, Mr. Edmonds can be reached at 888-229-5740 or by sending an email to redmonds@principiumgroup.com.

About The Principium Group

The Principium Group, Inc. is a leading advisory firm serving the green industry in the areas of mergers & acquisitions, exit planning and capital formation.

Principium professionals have assisted buyers and sellers in hundreds of transactions in a variety of industries, including consumer services, financial services, medical practices and others. They serve clients throughout North America.

Principium focuses on serving clients in the Green Industry, including landscape services, lawn maintenance, irrigation and related businesses. The Firm's professionals participate regularly in industry events and conferences.

Principium serves both buyers and sellers in mergers and acquisitions. For buyers, Principium provides assistance and counsel in strategic planning, identifying potential acquisition targets, conducting due diligence investigations and planning for successful integration of acquisitions. For sellers, Principium provides assistance and counsel in evaluating strategic alternatives, identifying and negotiating with potential acquirers and assisting with transactions from due diligence through the closing process. Principium also assists companies and their investors and financing sources with restructuring to achieve a profitable level of operations.

In addition to advising business buyers and sellers, The Principium Group provides educational material through its informational website SellMyGreenBusiness.com and its monthly electronic newsletter *Green Industry Merger & Acquisition News*. It also offers regularly scheduled workshops and seminars open to industry business leaders and offers custom-designed training for individual businesses and associations.

Principium professionals participate actively in key trade associations related to mergers & acquisitions, including the Association for Corporate Growth, the International Business Brokers Association and the Association of Professional Mergers & Acquisitions Advisors. Where appropriate, Principium cooperates with other organizations to bring the widest possible exposure to its clients. Their broad industry experience and background provides an advantage as companies plan for the future of your business, whether or not they are presently contemplating the sale of their business or adding to an existing business by acquiring another one. Principium Group professionals understand that the decision to sell a business is a profound decision for the owner.

Contact The Principium Group by email, telephone or on the web:

info@principiumgroup.com
888-229-5740
www.PrincipiumGroup.com.